Channeling Spirits

Clairaudience for Spirit World Communications

Gain a Wealth of Help!
Access the Collective Unconscious, Akashic Records, Spiritual
Guides, Life Purpose, Past Lives and More With Dowsing, Automatic
Writing, Guided Meditation and Real Examples

By Spirit Medium Laura

(aka Laura Bartolini Mendelsohn)

USA

www.SpiritMediumLaura.com

FREE OFFER

Get FREE "Channeling Spirit" Video Class Intro by joining
mailing list at **www.SpiritMediumLaura.com**

Disclaimer

This book is written to provide what the author believes to be, helpful tools and resources for learning how to channel. It is not in any way the only method to connect to spirit that works. There are as many unique methods as there are people.

The author has personally experienced excellent results following the tools and techniques outlined herein, however, does not and cannot, promise or guarantee any specific outcome.

A Note About Safety. It is advisable to ask in prayer only positive energy in love and light be addressed when working with spirit. Chapter one in this book explains how to do this.

About the Author

PSYCHIC MEDIUM & CLAIRVOYANT HEALER
SPIRIT MEDIUM LAURA
(aka LAURA BARTOLINI MENDELSOHN)

Seeing spirit uninvited as a child, Laura closed off until her master guide, St. Ignatius Loyola, (later discovered to be same as John of God) pushed through over 30 years ago. Some credentials include author of the Soul Psychic Healer Master Certification Program, featured as a top 100 Psychic in America in an authority publication, participates in after life research as a medium and is host of her own radio show. Laura has many more credentials described on her website here: www.SpiritMediumLaura.com.

Dedication

To my mother,

whose psychic presence in my life

encouraged my opening without restriction.

Thank you Mom.

To Theresa Jamund, my mother's friend,

who "knowingly and magically" gave me the book,

"The Game of Life," by Florence Skovell Shinn,

serendipitously awakening my natural gift as a psychic channel,

forever altering my identity and life path.

Thank you Tessi.

Introduction

This book offers gentle, simple development exercises to open your psychic sense of clairaudience (clear hearing), by channeling spiritual guides, light beings, angels, The Collective Unconscious (Akashic Records).

Once you make contact with your Divine Beings, your life will never be the same again. You will not be alone, in the dark or unassisted. It is like having your own private spiritual coach, ready to assist and help you through every step of your own life. Open your doorway and watch your miracles begin.

Everyone has their own unique way to connect. This book is constructed to gently guide the student forward with real life examples, simple development exercises, building to the next.

Contents

Chapter One: Pendulum and Spirit Board

What Are Spiritual Guides?

Your Spiritual Guides are here to help in your growth and spiritual evolution. While some individuals prefer to separate Angels from Spiritual Guides, in terms of incarnation on earth and function in the spiritual kingdom; I experience them in exactly the same way. They are evolved, intelligent light beings designed to help, heal and guide us on our paths.

How Do They Come In?

When I first started channeling my guides, I experienced them like a heavy energy which would caste itself upon me. My vocal chords would be taken over and I would channel them.

Now, when I ask my guides to come through, they feel like a light shift in energy. Then I start to ask them questions, usually in a silent telepathic way.

One day, as I worked with a client, I was asked to bring in the Metatron. The energy of Metatron was heavy, deep and very strong. In general, the feeling you have when you are channeling, will change according to the entity you are channeling.

Learning To Trust Your Guidance

When I was selling my condominium in Deerfield Beach, Florida a few years ago, the real estate market was in frenzy. Some homes sold before they were even put on the market, for prices higher than the seller was asking!

One morning after a meditation, I sat in communication with my Spiritual Guides. I asked about the correct price to sell my condominium. My spiritual guides stepped out of the way and brought in a soul who had recently deceased on earth.

This individual had been a real estate sales professional in my geographic location!

I sort of half believed in the validity of what I was receiving. I was told by this soul to ask for an astronomically high price for my condominium. She said there would be a person travelling from New York in the next month, who would pay cash for the unit. Therefore, I would not have to worry about having my property qualify in value for a mortgage at this higher asking price.

I thought that was interesting advice and at first advertised my condominium for sale at this price. However, within a few days I nervously lowered my asking price. I did not fully trust what I had been told by spirit. My condominium was sold a week later at this lower price.

About four weeks later, I ran into a neighbor of mine that had their condominium up for sale when I did. Their condominium was not quite as desirable as mine, however, it was comparable.

They told me they were able to sell their condominium for the exact price spirit told me to sell my unit at. They sold their condominium to a man from New York who paid cash for it!

I was mortified! If I had listened to spirit I would have been the one to sell at the much higher price to the purchaser from New York. I missed him by only a week's time!

Listen to your guidance, is the point of this story.

Who Are Spiritual Guides? (Channeled message from Alpha Omega Light Beings)

It is often asked of us in the spiritual realm, the non-physical realm, what is a spirit guide and why would anyone want one? We laugh at this, for it is obvious to us that to have contact with us will help you tremendously on your soul path on earth.

"What is your soul path," you might ask? We answer thusly:

Your soul path is the path you created with us, prior to your birth on Earth. We are here to help you find it again and to help you make good choices for yourself on Earth. These choices will lead to completion of your soul path.

Your soul path will provide for your greater awareness and a submission to something broader, wider and larger than you are. You soul path was planned so that you may live in an abundant flow and journey through life in a current of energy, that you planned prior to birth.

You soul path will help you achieve much in life. It will help you attain much on the material plane in particular, because your soul path is designed with abundance in mind. All things abundant will stem from it.

It was not designed to make you suffer, as some believe on Earth, especially in this time. Earth has evolved to a place energetically, at least the version of Earth in which you live, where souls are experiencing more and more material abundance.

Why? This is because Earth has become more like heaven, in vibration. The veil is lifting which separates us from you.

You are becoming more like us in frequency. So, now on Earth there is greater material wealth than before. At no time in history has there been such an amount of material abundance as there is today.

So, for you on Earth to open your awareness of your spiritual connection, you will open the floodgates to your prosperity as well.

God does not want you to suffer. God does not want anything for you actually.

What God wants, is that YOU BECOME MORE LIKE GOD and when you are more like God you are in abundance, right? Think about it. When you can create your life similar to God, you have found the Kingdom of Heaven on Earth.

This is what you are supposed to be doing on Earth during this timeframe.

In the past there were other types of growth on Earth, but abundance for the individual was not one of those things. There were times when piousness and devotion was the theme. Or, there were times when learning how to be fearless in the face of adversity was the theme.

That is not to say that these themes do not exist on Earth today, for on Earth there are all sorts of themes in play at the same time.

But the primary theme is abundance. This is the age of abundance and your veil has been lifted.

Now you ask, "What is a guide and why should I want one?"

First of all, the spiritual guide from the spirit world is designed to help you connect, on more than just an informational level. Once you make connection with us, you become more magnetic to attract wealth, true wealth and abundance on Earth.

What we mean by this is that we become a point of leverage for you to create your world as you like it. We give you more power to make your dreams come true on Earth.

How do we do this? Well, the first way is by helping you discover your soul dreams, not your ego dreams.

Soul dreams have supernatural power to them. Ego dreams do not. You can have anything you want on Earth; this is true, with enough work and mental focus.

However, to get spirit to work with you, your dreams must be for the evolution of mankind and other kinds (there are other species on Earth and in other dimensions of course) to help the whole.

The whole is vast and your idea of the whole is incomplete. The whole goes beyond other solar systems and other dimensions; it includes time lines and virtual realities, as well as, infinite possibilities.

When you become whole in what you affect, you reverberate wholeness to everyone and everything. Your vibration raises the total vibration of LOVE. This is why love is so important.

It is the only thing, the only energy, which can raise all other vibrations. LOVE is the key to prosperity my dear friend. LOVE is everything.

We do not suggest you enter the LOVE vibration so you can have more, "stuff." No. That is materialism for materialism's sake. We suggest you enter the LOVE vibration so you become more prosperous.

Prosperousness is beyond being material. Think about this. You can have much in terms of money, cash and things but what about soul? Is your soul nourished if you have a

Mercedes car? Your soul is not of the material world.

It is of the spiritual world and so, it is nourished better when you have LOVE.

LOVE is a feeling that you are connected to something greater than yourself. Love feels like you have the power and the peace of something so vast and so magnificent but you can only understand it when you are in it.

So your spiritual guides are here for you to experience true prosperity and live as your soul on Earth.

When you get in contact with your guides you will be able to manifest your desires easier, if they are soul level desires.

They are soul level desires when they help the whole.

So, service is emphasized there. When you decide you want to learn what your service on Earth is and then apply it, you will be led. The doors will be opened for you to the Kingdom of Heaven.

If you have not been getting results using so-called spiritual laws, like the Law of Attraction, it is because you have forgotten the service component to it.

You are not on Earth to have a great time. You are on Earth for service. So ask, "What is my service?" of your guides and see what the answer is.

You will be surprised that it is the thing you secretly yearn to do on Earth but did not know how to do. It is your secret dream for yourself that others would say is silly, impossible, or not practical.

This is your service. Your service always comes with imagined obstacles. We say imagined, because when you turn yourself into your service you will find that much will come of it. You will find the doors will open for you.

We want to help you because we are evolved souls; we have no other desire than to help other beings. It is our distinct joy to help.

When you align yourself with your distinct joy to help others, you will have our power to help you and you become powerful.

We do not say this to advertise that you should want to open your channel to the spiritual kingdom, so you have power but we do want to alert you to the fact that there is a reason for this.

It is not to get rich in the monetary sense. It is to get prosperous in the spiritual sense. Prosperity, will include money on Earth too, but is more than that. The money is incidental.

It is the service that counts.

So, even if you want to become a fashion model or a racecar driver, you will have much to learn about service on the path. Ask for the service and you will find the doors are going to open for you at light speed and the rewards are going to be monumental.

Ask that your service be revealed to you. This is the most important use of a spiritual guide and this is who we are.

God bless.

Tapping Into Your Spiritual Power (Article About How To Create A Pendulum)

This story reveals how to build your own pendulum, set up "yes" and "no" answers with it and finally, how to consult with one. As well, it alludes to the misuse of psychic tools. At times individuals can become very addicted to getting answers from the occult.

Spirit Answers To Heart Matters

Lorraine sat alone in her home, distraught. She had used up all her funds for calling online psychics. The love of her life, her ex-boyfriend, had rejected her. Today was the day he was moving in with his new girlfriend.

She was beside herself. Unable to let go and overspent on phone psychics, she decided to take out that dusty book from the shelf in her home, about using pendulums.

A little while ago, a friend of hers had said that using a pendulum was an excellent way to get answers to your own questions. So she decided to try.

The first thing the book told her was how to make her own pendulum. Here are the steps:

1. Take an 18" length of string.

2. Tie it to the end of a stone, pendant or some sort of weighted object.

3. Get the "yes" answer: Ask it a question to which you know the answer is "Yes." Watch the pendulum. The direction it goes in is the direction your pendulum will use when it wants to answer, "yes," to your question.

"Channeling Spirits" – Page 8

4. Get the "no" answer: Ask it a question to which you know the answer is "No." Watch the pendulum. The direction it goes in is the direction your pendulum will use when it wants to answer, "no," to your question.

She looked through her jewelry and found a beautiful pendant her ex-boyfriend had bought her. There on its chain, she readied to ask it a question. The first step was to ask it something that she already knew the answer to, in a "yes" or "no" format.

"Did it rain yesterday?" The pendulum slowly started to move back and forth almost as if it were shaking its head, saying, "No" to her. This was correct. It did not rain yesterday. So, Lorraine now knew how her pendulum would indicate the answer, "No."

"Am I wearing blue?" She asked the pendulum. The pendulum began circling slowly at first, but then began moving in a furiously fast, clockwise circle. She now knew the answer for, "Yes" as she was indeed wearing a blue dress that day.

Now she was ready to ask her most pointed question.

"Will Tom leave Melanie in less than a year?" The pendulum sat there shivering a bit without producing an answer. Then slowly, agonizingly slowly, the pendulum started to move in a clockwise circle.

Her answer had been presented. It was, "Yes."

Lorraine sat on her couch, momentarily ecstatic at the results. However, in a short time that lingering feeling of insecurity crept back into her belly.

She would have to find another way to get over losing her ex-boyfriend. Feverishly consulting the occult, was not a realistic or constructive using of her resources, although she thought the pendulum tool was excellent.

It was time for Lorraine to learn how to LOVE her situation, stop resisting it and open to the abundant flow of her life. As she sat there feeling anxious, a little voice began to speak in her head.

"Time to let go and let God, Lorraine," she heard in her head. She wondered if there was a way to attract love into her life in a more holistic and sustaining way. As she sat there, the phone rang.

It was a friend inviting her to attend an introductory lecture on, "The Secret to Luck." It was based on living intuitively, in accordance with the Law of Attraction. She decided maybe the spiritual truths of this class would help her. She agreed to go.

Becoming addicted to psychic answers is the sign an individual needs healing, not a reading. Aligning with your soul's path and service is a good place to start to heal your addictions, connect to the LOVE vibration, and become prosperous again.

Building Your Own Tools: Pendulums and Spirit Boards

It is very easy to build your own pendulum, to get answers from spirit in a way that goes beyond your conscious mind.

One of the most difficult skills to acquire, when developing psychically, is to learn how to "get out of your way." This is especially true if you are doing readings for yourself.

Usually we are very emotionally attached to a particular outcome. I know for myself if I try to channel my Spiritual Guides on a subject of which I am highly attached, it is almost impossible to get "clear," uninfluenced results.

A Pendulum or a Spirit Board, (more on this below) is a great way to get around this, somewhat. It is not perfect, but is helpful.

The following are instructions on how to create and use your own Pendulum.

Steps To Create A Simple Pendulum

1. Get an 18 inch piece of thread.
2. Get a paper clip.
3. Tie the thread to the edge of the paper clip.
4. Ask the pendulum a fact of which you know the answer to be, "no." Wait to see where the pendulum goes. This is your "no" symbol from the pendulum.
5. Ask the pendulum a question of which you know the answer to be, "yes." Wait to see the pendulum move. The direction in which it moves is your "yes" movement from thependulum.

6. Prepare to work with your Pendulum by first doing the LOVE formula as outlined on next page.

7. Ask the pendulum a question you need an answer to in your life.

8. Watch the pendulum move.

9. This is your answer.

Buy A Pendulum

You can buy pendulum from your preferred New Age supply retailer, should you prefer to do so.

Using a Dowsing Chart With Your Pendulum

When you get really good at using your pendulum, you might want to try using it with a dowsing, or pendulum chart. There are many to be found prepared on the Internet by Googling for, "pendulum chart copyright free." The following chart was found in this way.

Steps to use Your Pendulum with a Dowsing Chart

1. After preparing with the LOVE formula, ask your pendulum a question.

"Channeling Spirits" – Page 13

2. Move the pendulum over the board.

3. When it starts moving in a yes pattern you have found the answer, or part of the   answer.

4. Record what comes through.

5. You might get letters that spell out a word, or you may just get the "yes" or "no" answer this way.

Buy a Dowsing Chart

You can buy a dowsing chart from your preferred New Age supply store.

Working With Spirit Boards: A Note About Safety.

Many have said an "Ouija" board is very unsafe and can open a portal to lower astral vibrations, troubled spirits and negative energy. This is very true, but it is true of all spirit work.

This is why it is important to always use the LOVE formula as outlined on next page, before doing any spirit work.

The L-O-V-E Formula

Before you can use the Pendulum, or any other form of spirit contact, you need to prepare to ensure the best results. I call this the LOVE formula.

I created the LOVE formula, as a way for you to have an exact formula to **safely** access the spirit world and mind of the universe. Without a consistent technique, your results will be unpredictable and unreliable.

It includes a section on how to get to the slower brain wave state of theta, which really is the key to all of this.

Here it is:

1. Let go in meditation.

    a. Theta Brain Wave Meditation. The most important secret to opening your miracle mind, is through deliberate access to deep Alpha to Theta brain wave states. It is this brain wave state, which is responsible for access to the miracle mind, collective unconscious, or what physicists call, "zero point." (More information on this follows below.)

    b. The easiest way I have found to gain access to this brain wave state, is to use a "Deep Theta Meditation," which can be found for free on www.YouTube.com. If you do this daily, or before working psychically, you will have a significant advantage.

    c. You will need at least eight minutes of listening.

    d. We enter Theta every day doing ordinary activities

such as day dreaming, watching a boring TV show, listening to a dull lecture, in the shower, walking, driving a long distance on a straight, desolate highway, staring at a hypnotic spiral wheel, reading an absorbing book, deep in meditation and during sleep. More information about Theta Trance is in the next section.

2. Open in prayer. "Father, mother, god, all beings of the highest light and love, please come to me now in the reading for 'name.' Please allow all messages to be received clearly, accurately, as intended for the highest good and benefit of 'name' and all those with whom he/she comes in contact. Please allow us to only work in the highest love, light and protected vibration. And so it is."

3. Align with the vibration of your subject by visualizing your energy fields combining.

   a. Visualize yourself sitting opposite your subject, (person for which you are reading). If that subject is already in front of you, then simply see them in your mind's eye.

   b. Imagine they have an energy field coming out of them.

   c. Imagine you have an energy field coming out of yourself.

   d. Imagine both energy fields blending.

   e. You should feel a click as you connect.

4. Entirely receive.

   a. Entirely receiving is the most difficult phase of

this process for many people, but is critical to be able to do, in order to access your miracle mind. You must be willing to allow yourself to report, or accept anything that comes in as part of your psychic experience, even if it seems silly.

i. Example. I was doing mediumship for a client. I had tried to bring in her mother at our first session. Instead, someone by the name of Christine came in, who had died about six months prior of uterine cancer.

She appeared with short brown hair, a fair complexion and spoke about her two grandchildren. This was my client's aunt. Everything that came in was exactly correct.

When I tried to bring in the mother of my client right after this, the material was foggy, unclear and imprecise.

We tried on another occasion to bring in her mother. However, this time something new happened.

As her mother tried to talk to us, a tall man interrupted the communication. He was wearing a western style shirt and hat. He was light in coloring with blond hair. He said to me, "We are from the west. We are from the west."

At first, I felt strange to deliver this seemingly meaningless message to my client, but did nevertheless.

My client laughed. Her mother's maiden name was West. The man that appeared was her maternal grandfather, offering validating information so my client would know we were indeed in contact with her family.

So, you see if you do not allow spirit to speak to you completely, you will fail. As a matter of fact, if you do not report all the information you get from a psychic session completely, your flow will be blocked.

So, go ahead and report what you get fearlessly. You will be rewarded!

Remember to Be Positive

One of the biggest challenges a spiritual messenger can have is delivering an alarming message to the sitter (one receiving the messages). The best way to do this is by being honest in a positive way.

For example if you receive a message from spirit that the sitter possibly has heart disease, suggest a visit to the doctor for a thorough physical checkup rather than saying that person definitely is ill.

Ways to Slow Your Brain Waves

There are many ways to slow down our brain waves, most of which you do not need to think about. We do move in and out of the miracle consciousness of slower brain waves daily. The most common of these methods is through dreaming.

Benefits of Theta Trance

Increased learning capability, creativity, out of body experience, lucid dreaming, relief of stress, communication with your subconscious mind for hypnosis, heightened energy, faster healing, psychic development and a more astute memory.

Ways To Go To Theta

It is recommended to use one of the www.YouTube.com theta meditations for at least 7 to 8 minutes, when you are told to meditate. This is the primary way I meditate as of the writing of this book.

If this is not helping you go deep enough, then purchase a full, thirty minutes theta meditation audio from a good New Age retailer.

Here's how to enter a slower brain wave state for spirit work:

1. www.YouTube.com has various meditations you can watch for FREE, online.

2. Any type of visual focus for five to ten minutes. Use an online timer for this like www.e.ggtimer.com.

   a. Focusing on a candle, picture, plant, etc. Watching TV.

b. Closing your eyes, focusing on your visual field, especially at the space between your eyebrows.

c. Sunset Meditations from www.YouTube.com.

d. Hypnotic Spiral. You can find one online. Keep your mind clear as you stare at this hypnotic spiral. This spiral helps you connect with the infinite, since a spiral is a sacred geometry symbol, which stands for unification with source.

3. Staring at computer for long periods of time.

4. Driving on a long, monotonous road.

5. Listening to someone boring, or being in a boring class.

6. Meditation. Deep TM.

7. Brain wave entrainment <u>technology</u>. Often easier to use. Isochronal tones, you can learn to increase your production of theta brainwaves and experience their benefits for yourself.

Steps to Create Your Own "Spirit Board"

1. Print out a royalty free Dowsing or Pendulum Chart from the Internet. The following chart was found by, "Googling" for "Pendulum Chart copyright free."

2. Place this chart under a piece of glass. A glass, topped frame is a good way to do this.

3. Get yourself a shot glass, or a small juice glass.

4. Turn it upside down.

5. You now have the equipment needed to do spirit board work.

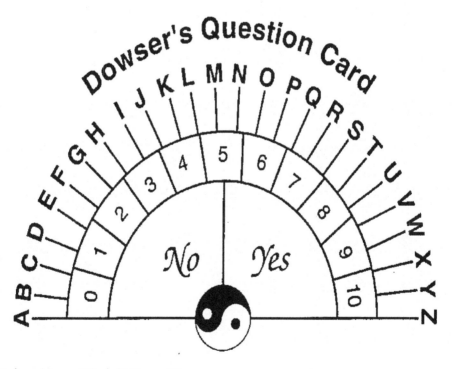

Using Your "Spirit Board"

1. Prepare with the LOVE formula. REMEMBER TO ASK

FOR PROTECTION!

2. Turn your glass upside down.

3. Ask your question.

4. Allow the glass to move on top of the board.

5. It will spell out answers of just give you a "yes" or "no" answer.

6. Make a note of what answer appears.

Buy A Spirit Board

Should you prefer to buy a professionally manufactured Spirit Board you can find one at most New Age retailers.

What to Ask Your Spiritual Guides

You can ask your guides many questions. Keep in mind your Spiritual Guides are here to help you grow in this lifetime, complete your life purpose and achieve your greatness.

It is not wise to consult with them as you would a fortune teller. They usually will tell you they are not here to tell you what to do. They are not here for that purpose.

Most importantly, your Spiritual Guides are here to help you evolve spiritually. So the more you ask questions related to your growth, the better your answers will be.

Here are some sample questions to ask your Spiritual Guides:

1. Am I on my path?
2. Is the relationship I am in with "name," a good one for my soul path and development?
3. Will I get married in this lifetime? Have children?
4. What are their names?
5. Do I have any untapped talents I am supposed to use in this lifetime?
6. How many times have I been incarnated?
7. When will I be able to stop incarnating?
8. Is there such a thing as incarnation?
9. Can I know my "name" from another lifetime?
10. What did I do in my past lifetime? Who was I?
11. Did we know each other in another lifetime?
12. Are there Angels?

13. What is the next step on my soul path in this lifetime?

You can also ask questions about your life. However, expect a loving, higher level response than a "fortune telling" one.

1. Will my ex-boyfriend "name" come back to me?

    Answer: your guides will tend to speak about why you are in the relationship, what is supposed to happen in it from a growth and love perspective and how you can handle it for the highest good of all involved. They will tend not to try to tell you how to manipulate him, to get him back. If you receive this type of message, you are working with a lower level energy, which should be avoided.

2. How do I handle the controlling nature of my mother?

    Answer: Spirit will explain to you why your mother acts the way she does and provide to you some helpful ways to deal with the situation, which are loving to you and her. Spirit will not say your mother is "evil," or in any way be negative. If you receive a negative answer you are working with a lower level energy, not a spiritual guide.

3. Should I go into business with "name"?

    Answer: Spirit will be able to tell you if this on your soul path, how it matches, or does not match the service you have come to Earth to do and what the outlook for your success, within this business is. If you are told something like, "this business will help you get rich and rule the world," you are probably working with a lower level energy, which should be avoided.

How to Ask Negative Energy To Leave

First of all, let it suffice to say, I have not had problems with negativity coming into my spirit contact. As soon as you desire to work with spirit, your guides will rally to the occasion and protect you. At least this is my belief and has been my experience.

However, to ensure protection use the LOVE formula. Built into the prayer is a request for protection.

If an entity talks from a perspective of evil, mean or cruel competitive ideas, you are working with a lower astral type of energy. You will want to ask that entity to go away and ask your guides to provide protection for you.

Here is a sample script to use:

Dear Spiritual Guides, please escort this negative energy away from me right now. Please allow me to work only in a protected space of white light. (Repeat two more times.) I thank you in advance for your help. Amen.

Exercises

Use Your Pendulum to Get Answers

Think of a current problem you are having in your life. You have tried fixing it yourself and no matter what you do, you still do not have a firm grip on a solution.

Now, turn to your pendulum for the answer. Use either the pendulum you made yourself or one you purchased.

1. Prepare with the LOVE formula as described above.

2. Think of a way to ask for guidance from spirit in a "yes" or "no" answer format.

3. Ask your question and receive the answers.

4. Do this for a friend too.

Using Your Spirit Board To Get Answers

Think of a problem you are having in your life, or find a friend that needs guidance.

Now turn to your Spirit Board for the answer. You can either use one you purchased, or the one you created yourself.

1. Prepare with the LOVE formula as described above.

2. Ask your question and receive the answers.

Meet Your Guides Using Pendulum and Spirit Board

Now it is time to begin communicating with your very own Spiritual Guides using the pendulum and spirit board. Here are the steps.

1. Prepare with the LOVE formula.

2. Ask your guides using both the Pendulum and Spirit Boards, the following questions:

    a. Did we know each other in another lifetime?

    b. Have you always been in my life in this incarnation?

    c. Have we ever-reversed roles, where I was your guide in another lifetime and you were on Earth?

    d. Any of the questions delineated earlier in the Chapter in the Section, "What to Ask Your Spiritual Guides."

Keep working with the spirit board and the pendulum until you feel a sense of fluidity. At this time you will then be ready to move to Chapter Two, which is about Automatic Writing.

Chapter Two: Automatic Writing - Who's Moving Your Pen?

One of the most wonderful ways to channel, is to learn how to allow spirit to come through you as you write. This is called automatic writing.

The Creative Process is Channeling

Acting, singing, dancing, painting, sculpting, creative writing are all aspects of channeling. Taken in its broadest sense, channeling allows something larger than our ego driven, beta mind to surface. Channeling is flow.

If you read my first book, "Manifesting Magic: The 'Soul Abundance' Law of Attraction Secret," you have already been introduced to the concept of living your life in harmony with a higher power. When you learn how to Let Go of control, Open to your secret dream, Vibrationally align to your dream and Entirely receive what comes in, you are in flow.

This is exactly what the creative process and channeling are. If you want to become more creative, learn how to flow; then learn how to channel.

Channeling feels like something other than our conscious mind is sending intelligence through us.

Trance versus Conscious Channeling

You should be in at least some form of a light trance when you channel. I have provided resources in Chapter One about how to enter Theta Trance state. Use this resource to choose a method you enjoy to enter trance state, when you attempt to channel.

Concepts about Channeling

1. You do not need to be completely unconscious to do automatic writing. This class will focus on conscious writing.

2. Automatic writing can feel like someone else is doing the physical act of writing. Some mediums have even written in unconscious states, as another consciousness moved their pen.

3. In contrast, this class will focus on conscious writing. You will feel like you are doing something. The thoughts that come through, however, will feel as if they originated from somewhere other than your own brain.

Your Guides versus Higher Self

Some individuals wonder if they are getting information from their higher self, or their spiritual guides. I have personally experienced that both feel the same, so it is best to ask when you make contact, whether you are speaking to Spiritual Guides or higher self.

I have experienced speaking to loved ones in spirit as well, because my Spiritual Guides brought them in during automatic writing sessions as they needed to answer specific, earth related questions.

I think the easiest way to understand all of this, is to realize there really is only one consciousness. This is the super conscious mind of God. So there really is no need to discern if you are speaking to your spirit guide, higher consciousness or a

deceased human being, unless you feel it is absolutely
necessary. If you do, just ask. You will get a very clear answer.

Once you make contact with your Spiritual Guides, all the
communications will begin to blend and soon you will not even
ask. This is how it is for me.

The Difference Between Your Guides And Your Higher Self

As I have already stated, it is not really needed for you to know
the difference for Channeling to be helpful or accurate. After a
while, you will have spirit communications from different
sources.

All you need to do is ask and the right source will be instantly
delivered to you.

It is important to note however, that sometimes the right source
is not the one you requested. If that is the case spirit will let
you know and deliver the correct mind that should speak to
you.

The Secret To Channeling

The point here is that the key, or secret to Channeling, is not a
Pendulum, Spirit Board, automatic writing, vocal box or other
external thing. These are tools for connection. The secret is the
connection, made with the right brain wave state.

This entire course will pivot on how we can train the brain to
slow down its waves at will, raising our ability to sense faster,
lighter frequencies we might miss if we were in normal beta
brain state.

When the brain waves slow down, you can sense finer

vibrations.

Spirit Slows Down

It is not only our human responsibility to make this connection. Spirit has a role in it as well. When spirit decides it will work with you, it will slow down its frequency to intercept your brain waves. Even when we are in deep Theta brain wave state, spirit still does have to slow down its vibration to make the handshake of contact.

This course is training you to slow down your brain wave state during meditation. Then go through various exercises to help you make that connection to your spiritual guides. Once you have that connection, you will have access to your own personal spiritual coaches, as well as be able to coach and counsel others with their guides.

Spirit is a wonderful resource. Welcome to it.

How To Slow Down Your Brain Waves

The main method to slow down brain waves is meditation. You might have heard stories of individuals who, in deep meditation, began to communicate with their Spiritual Guides.

Others who practice Out of Body Experiences, or Lucid Dreaming techniques are slowing down their brain waves.

The most desirable brain wave state is to resonate in a continuum from deep Alpha to light Theta. Brain waves in this range will give you the most complete experience.

Since we are usually asleep when we are in Theta brain wave state, the objective is to go to Theta and still remain awake. Then we can operate our minds at a slower brain wave level to connect to a higher frequency for the best level of accuracy.

Can Anyone Gain Access To His or her Spiritual Guides, Or Do You Have To Be Chosen? (Channeled Material From Alpha Omega Light Beings)

You do not have to be chosen, you have to choose. If you truly want and desire spirit contact, you will gain it. This is not a skill held only for a privileged few. It is available for all to learn and to use.

So, if someone tells you that you are not talented enough to do this, they are incorrect. You can do this and your desire to do this automatically qualifies you.

Remember, you would not feel like you want to do this unless you had the ability to do it. If you were of a different frequency, which would make spirit communications difficult, then you would not desire to do it. You chose to do spirit communications prior to birth and so therefore, you brought in the right equipment to do so.

God bless.

Making First Contact

My first contact with the world of spirit happened when I was very young. I think I was about three to five years old.

After my mother would put me to sleep at night, I would have terrifying experiences. As my brain waves slowed down, from beta to alpha to theta, I would begin to hear the soft sound of voices off in the distance. Then they would get louder and louder until they changed into a loud buzzing noise, which was unbearable in its intensity.

At this point, the noise would suddenly be followed by dead silence, only to be filled again with the voices and faces of people I didn't know!

At times, a wise old man would present himself to me. He would make me feel a bit better, but only for a short while. No matter how wise and loving this being was, I inevitably would begin to scream in terrified subjection.

After all, I was just a little girl. If spirit was trying to speak to me, it had to remember I was now a human being on Earth. I did not remember the spirit world, or that it was safe and normal to talk to my Spiritual Guides.

Near Death Spirit Help

At about this time, around four years of age, my parents rented a bungalow in upstate New York during the summer. Since I was raised in a loose and free way, I tried to teach myself how to swim, in the community lake.

I remember looking at the adults to see what they did and trying to imitate them. After a failed attempt, I drifted down under the water. As I sat there on the bottom, I remember thinking how it was down there. I decided to breathe in the water, to see if I could live there.

Obviously, I was just a young child without knowledge of danger. As I began to breathe in the water, I heard that loud buzzing noise I usually heard at night. I saw a white light come in from my right visual field and then finally I heard this loud command, "Get out!"

As I heard the command, a strong energy propelled me up and forward, toward the shore. As I ran out of the water to my mother I fumbled my explanation, too excited to find the right words. How could a four year old explain to her mother this had happened?

Teenage Ruminations

Although I did not know this then, I had spirit contact during my teenage years. I think rather than call it spirit contact, I will call it "light being" contact.

After doing some research, I have found mention of souls who came to Earth to help with the 2012 ascension. They are from other star systems and dimensions. I think I am one of these individuals.

Just today I did some research on the loud buzzing noise in my ears and what, if any, supernatural experiences others who experience similar sounds, might have had. I found there are "Star Seeds," to whom I clearly relate, who hear such sounds. As of this writing such phenomenon is discussed at this location:

www.angelfire.com/ok/innerradiance/starwanderers.html

In addition, the lucid dreaming and out of body experience community, clearly admits to, "loud buzzing sounds" or "the party sound" just before leaving the body, or having a lucid dream.

I believe the loud buzzing sound is the brain waves slowing down to connect to a higher vibration or frequency, where paranormal experiences can be obtained.

My Teenage Contact

As a teenager I was very drawn to meditation, the sky, the stars and consciousness. I mentioned above, I believe I am a Star Seed. It was only natural for me to listen to "Sounds From Space" radio, then allow myself to "travel."

I never was attracted to taking drugs. So, understand this was an innocent fifteen year old, who only desired to expand her consciousness.

During these drug free trips, I would be taken into the stars and taught things. It was the most fun an introverted, intuitive, shy, sensitive, bookish type of teenager could have.

I would turn on the music and allow it to fill me. I would become one with the music, no thought involved whatsoever. As I lay on my bed, I suddenly would feel like I was flying. At this point I would receive something that felt like a download of mathematical and spiritual concepts.

One of the most profound truths I was taught, was the concept of infinity. I had just learned about it in math class, so it was fresh in my impressionable mind.

I am going to try to describe what was taught to me.

The universe is infinite in all directions. The number of universes is infinite. There is no smallest point or largest point. There is no fixed reality. Everything is always changing in all directions.

The universe is a symphony of vibrations. It never rests. It is not fixed.

This is how spirit contact can be. Get ready for your own adventure with it, particularly if you start experimenting with different methods of meditation and mind entrainment.

This was not yet vocal contact with my guides. However, it was a form of contact.

Vocal Contact Made

Exactly fifteen years and much ado about nothing later, I arrived at a time in my life where I was laid off from work. I had an extremely boring, systems consulting job. Software came easily to me but held no promise of mystery to feed and nourish my naturally adventurous self.

My mother had a friend, Theresa Jamund, who gave me a prosperity classic to read. It is called, "The Game of Life and How to Play It," by Florence Scovel Shinn. It is still available for purchase, although originally published in the early 1920s.

The book essentially states, if you follow your intuition you will be led to your prosperous purpose. Due to this time off from work, I had free time and had developed a meditative balance in my life. So, one day I decided to try what the book suggested you do.

The book said, to follow your intuitive flow. That day I left my Queens, New York apartment, hopped on the subway, ended up in New York Central Park next to a stranger. We began to speak.

It turned out he was regularly going to a famous psychic medium in Manhattan during the 1980s. I no longer remember the medium's name as this was quite some time ago. But I do remember he had about 18 aged Siamese cats, some of which would languidly join us for the most remarkable trance mediumship demonstrations I ever saw.

My new friend invited me to go with him to meet a psychic reader in northern Manhattan. The reader had a heavy Cuban Spanish accent, his walls adorned with pictures of saints with dried flowers and offerings to them.

He quickly laid out a tarot spread for me, too warn to see the card art any longer. After peering at them a moment, he told me my guides were trying to come through. I raced home to see what would happen if I asked them to visit. I was NOT disappointed

As soon as I closed the door behind me to my 600 square foot apartment, I asked for my Spiritual Guides to come through. My head was thrown back from my neck. A deep and frightening voice began to speak.

I was petrified and attempted to run away in fear. Unfortunately (or fortunately?), my little apartment was so small I had nowhere to run!

However, curiosity got the better of me and I asked again. Before you knew it, I was having a grand old time channeling my guides.

For the first two weeks, I had a guide by the name of "Michael," come through. He stayed with me until he said I was ready to meet my day-to-day guide, named Ola. It took two weeks.

Ola is still with me as part of a team. I found out a month or so later, as I was curious, asking spirit for an explanation, Ola is short for St. Ignatius Loyola. I thought that was nice, but had no idea at that time that St. Ignatius Loyola was and still is the Master Guide to John of God, famed Brazilian healer!

My channeling has developed into psychic mediumship and readings for clients, as well as a spiritual practice. The guides have authored the Soul Abundance material, through me.

Soul Abundance, is the way to awaken your power by following your heart. If you want to live your dreams, you have to let go of controlling your life, be open to doing what you love, vision it and then entirely receive it. This is the LOVE formula for living your dreams.

Earlier in this book, I reviewed the LOVE formula for channeling. The steps are essentially the same as those for Soul

Abundance, but adapted to the act of spirit contact, through channeling.

Exercises

In order to get ready to do automatic writing, it is helpful to do some warm up exercises. You may do these exercises over and over again, until you are able to do automatic writing without them.

Music – Drawing Warm-up

Supplies: A theta meditation, soul inspiring piece of music and a piece of paper and pencil, or pen.

Directions: After doing a Theta Meditation for 8 to 10 minutes, (Chapter One) you will be ready to begin.

Play some music that is soul inspiring to you.

Listen to the music, attempting to "feel" it. After you begin to "feel" the music, begin to draw on your piece of paper anything you feel. Anything you draw is correct, so long as you communicate your feelings about the music, through the drawing.

It is important to allow the music to move the pencil or pen over the paper and to not think about what you are doing. Just allow the music to inspire you.

Now begin the Automatic Writing Exercise.

Automatic Writing

Take out a pad and pen and set it beside you. Begin to write about a situation in your life that needs healing, or resolution, or advice. Write down everything you can think of about the subject.

Now, write a question about this situation to which you do not know the answer. Sit and wait for an answer to come to you.

Write it down.

If an answer does not come to you, begin to write the words, "The answer is" and wait to see what you get. If you still do not get an answer write down, "it is easy to handle this because" and allow the rest to flow out of you.

If you still do not get an answer then write, "the answer is to relax and" and then write what you hear. If none of these attempts bring you an answer, then it is fine to just let go of the process today and try tomorrow, after doing the above warm up.

In the next chapter, you will be learning some extensive and very powerful ways to open yourself to vocal channeling.

The key to all of this, is to learn how to let go of trying to answer the questions yourself. Allow something else to come through.

Other Questions to Ask Your Spiritual Guides

How many Spiritual Guides do I have?

What is the purpose of our connection, in this lifetime?

Do I have a soul mate here on earth?

Chapter Three: Channeling Your Life Purpose

In this chapter we are going to focus on two things. The first, is making vocal contact with your guides. The second, is to learn about our life purpose.

Once you get very good at automatic writing, it should be fairly easy to simply channel your guides vocally. It is a good idea to learn how to do this, especially if you are going to give messages to others, for clients do expect to hear the messages directly.

The key to getting information from your guides, is to keep your mind open about what you receive. Even the seemingly silly could be important.

When I first asked spirit about a past life of my sister's, which was important to her current life, I received the most interesting but easily doubtable, information.

I was told that my sister had been a Maia Goddess, then spirit spelled it for me! They said it was spelled M-A-I-A not M-A-Y-A-N as in Mexican Mayan religion.

I was told that my sister was a Priestess who healed people and animals with herbal remedies. Around her I saw goats and other animals. She lived in caves in the southern mountainous regions of what is now Italy.

They showed me a mental picture of her wearing a long white

robe with a gold sash around the middle. She wore a piece of gold jewelry, which spiraled, around her upper left arm.

As soon as I was able, I went to research this information. Apparently, the Maian were the Roman counterpart of the Greek Gaian religion. The information was confirmed!

If you "Google" for "the gaia religion in italy is maia " you will find information about this connection. As of the writing of this book here is the first listing from that Google search from Wikipedia.

In an archaic Roman prayer Maia was explicitly identified with Earth (Terra, the Roman counterpart of Gaia) and the Good Goddess (Bona Dea). Her identity became theologically intertwined also with the goddesses Fauna, Magna Mater ("Great Goddess", referring to the Roman form of Cybele but also a cult title for Maia).

Incidentally, my sister and I are of Italian origin this life time, making this "hit" even more connected.

So, how do you get information this relevant from spirit? Here is a detailed answer about how to develop your vocal channeling skills from Spiritual Guides.

Dear Spiritual Guides, What is the Best Way to Vocally Channel Spiritual Guides?

As we have said earlier in this book, it is important to take time every day to rest and be in contemplation. It is only in this way you will begin to have spirit contact with our dimension. We are of a higher, or faster vibration than yours, so it is important for you to slow down to lift up.

Slowing down is the key to making connection.

There are other things to learn as well. Many individuals who come to earth at this time, are trying to open up their throat chakra, which stands for expression of their mission, or life purpose. They are trying to learn what their mission is and then to express it. So, it is important to work on the throat chakra in various exercises of self-expression, vocally.

Singing, for example, is an excellent choice for one to develop to channel successfully. It does not seem a likely choice but nevertheless, if you were to begin to learn how to sing, you would suddenly open your heart and throat chakras at the same time. Singing is based in these chakras.

It is emotion and it is expression, directly from the soul. The most moving singers on earth are very connected to their heart and know how to express what is in it, beautifully.

If you do not fancy yourself a singer, it is easy to develop this chakra anyway by toning. Yes, every morning after or during a meditation on the throat chakra you can tone, or emit sounds from your throat that are pleasant.

Tone from the lowest note to the highest. It important to pick seven frequencies each time you do this.

So, if you are starting low then slowly escalate to higher and higher notes until you have reached the seventh note, which should be the highest. Then you start over but in reverse. Do it at least once a day, from low to high and then from high to low. It is best if you do it seven times a day, for seven days.

After you have done this for seven days in succession, you are now ready to use words. Words that flow naturally from you as you are toning.

You can start with any words that appeal to you or pick one to start such as the word, "love." This then becomes an active meditation from the throat chakra.

Start to, "sing" the word "love" at your lowest tone, then slowly move it up the scale seven times. Then, start from your highest note and slowly move down the scale seven times in total. Do this for seven more days.

Finally, you are ready to start channeling words. Start with the word you just used, which was "love," for the lowest tone. Then change the word to something else.

It could be, "bird," "root," "like," "feel." The important thing is that you now begin to change the words.

Do this up the scale seven times and then down the scale seven times. Do this for seven days.

Now to Channel

At this point you should feel very, very comfortable allowing words to flow from your throat chakra in a relaxed way. Now it is time to channel your guides.

Take an eight minute Theta Meditation, obtainable for free from www.YouTube.com. It is very, very easy to find meditations on

Youtube that you will like, those that will put you in a theta brain wave state.

Now, after doing your meditation it is time to begin to channel your guides.

Sit in a comfortable location. Ask your guides to come to you with this prayer:

"Dear Spiritual Guides, please come to me now in love and light, for a session. I give thanks in advance that messages come through clearly, accurately and as intended for the highest good of all. Thank you."

Now sit and wait for a feeling to enter your body. You should feel something coming into your sphere of energy, from the upper right part of your head. It usually will feel like a click, or a shift of energy.

If you do not feel anything, this is fine, too. Some people do not notice a feeling. Now ask a question of your guides.

Here is a great question to ask: "What am I here to do in this lifetime?" Wait for the answer. Speak out loud any thoughts that come into your mind. These thoughts are your guides speaking to you.

Continue with this method for at least 15 minutes on your first try.

If nothing comes through that is intelligible, try using the "Contacting Your Spiritual Guides Meditation" that follows below.

Then ask your guides questions.

Meditation To Meet Your Spiritual Guides and Learn About Past Lives – Channeled

Background Sounds:

This meditation is particularly effective if you play the sound of the ocean in the background. You can find one agreeable to yourself by searching on: www.YouTube.com.

I recorded this meditation for you at this link: www.spiritmediumlaura.com/meetdivinebeing.wma

If you would like to record your own version of this, you can do so very simply on your computer. Go here to read how: www.wikihow.com/Record-Your-Voice-on-a-Computer

Perhaps I will get these meditations professionally recorded for purchase in the future, but for now these are your resources.

Meditation Starts Here:

Take a couple of deep breaths to relax, pushing away any tension or anxiety on the exhale. Take your attention to the skin on your forehead. Feel it relax. It might feel a little numb, that's good.

Now feel the skin on your neck and shoulders. Imagine it feels a little numb. Relax and you feel it. Take your attention to your arms and hands. Can you feel them getting heavy and tingling? Good. Now go to your torso. Imagine it is filled with water and is very heavy. Now feel it tingling. Good. Go to your thighs. Feel how heavy they are and numb. Good.

Feel your calves and feet. They are so heavy. Feel them tingle. Good.

Imagine yourself at the ocean. You are totally relaxed. As you stare at the sea you look up and down the beach. You decide to walk in one direction. Turn in that direction and begin walking.

Pay attention to what you see.

Without straining, just relax and look about.

What do you notice as you casually stroll slowly down the beach?

Notice the colors, shapes, objects and textures you see.

Continue to breathe slowly while walking at a comfortable relaxed pace, just enjoying the stroll, letting the images come to you gently.

Listen to the breeze, to the calling birds, whatever sounds are there. What can you hear as you stroll along?

Take a deep breath in.

You see a forest off to your right. You feel very drawn to walk into the forest. When you arrive at the entrance, you notice a path. You enter.

The forest is beautiful inside. Large green leaves, ferns, flowers and you hear birds and other animals. Just enjoy yourself as you move forward. What else do you feel, hear and see as you follow the path?

Keep walking, slowly strolling, enjoying the walk down this path.

Feel the weather, feel the clothes on your body, feel what is around you. Notice the temperature. Continue to stroll forward.

You are being led to walk in a particular direction. Suddenly, you notice there is a clearing up ahead. You are drawn to walk towards it. The forest is ending and there is an open expanse with a small, ancient cottage.

The cottage is in excellent shape, even though it is very old. It is made of stone with a thatched roof.

As you draw closer to this cottage, you notice the door to it is very unusual. It is a different shape, color and size than most doors. What does your door look like?

When you arrive at this door, you knock on it. No one answers.

You knock again. The door starts to creak open a bit. You push on it and it opens.

In the house across the room is a large window with a table under it. There is a figure seated at the table wearing a robe. You cannot see the face of the person in the robe but you know this is a benevolent being, waiting to meet you.

The walls of the room are made of rocks and stone. It is beautiful, clean and very, very old. You are drawn to go sit on the other chair at the table, facing this robed individual.

You go there. When you arrive you hear the words, "Pay attention" in your head. Suddenly, the robe starts to melt away and there is your special spiritual guide, the one who is assigned to work with you today.

You say, "Hello."

Your spiritual guide says, "Hello" back. There is a smile between you and a feeling of deep familiarity, benevolence and love.

Imagine your guide is made up of light and this light is gently extending into the room. Also, your light is extending into the room until both of you connect energetically.

You should feel a click as this happens.

Do it one more time to be sure.

Now we are going to ask our spiritual guide the following questions:

Dear Spirit Guide, what is my purpose in this lifetime?

Your Spiritual Guide looks at you with a kind, knowing and benevolent gaze. At first you do not hear, see or feel an answer, then all of a sudden you are given an answer.

Take a moment to receive what comes in. It could be a feeling, you could see something, or you might hear a string of words, which describe your life purpose. Just pay attention to what you get.

Now you are going to slowly open your eyes and record what you received. Record everything without leaving even the slightest detail out.

Anything you receive has value.

You may repeat this exercise as much as you like. Each day you do it you will receive more information, until you have a complete story.

Here is a channeled piece from The Alpha Omega on how to find your life purpose, or mission and why you would want to do so.

Dear Spiritual Guides, why is it important to know our life purpose and how can we find it out?

The biggest problem for people on earth is the heart. Each individual on earth has come with a mission to complete. Their mission is to heal their heart.

So, the biggest problem for people on earth is to heal their heart, how they feel about themselves, their life and others.

Many people think the biggest problem people have is with other people, as in love or with other things such as money. No. The biggest problem people have is their relationship with themselves relating to love, or money, or relating to a relationship with others and material things.

So when you heal yourself, you heal your entire life from love to money.

We are going to give you a simple test to perform on yourself to find your mission in life. When you find your mission, you will have something to focus on about yourself.

When you get going on your mission, you are beginning the self-healing process. When you heal yourself, your relationship with others and things will improve.

You will enter a state of infinite harmony with the universe.

You cannot be in harmony with the external world, until you have entered into harmony with your own internal world. You have to be at peace with yourself.

You have to know why you have come to earth. Then you need to open to this mission.

The mission could be as simple as self-acceptance but this is your mission. It could be as complex as becoming a world leader.

When you accept your mission, you accept yourself and you become very, very peaceful.

When you become peaceful, your miracles begin to blossom. It is through self-peace that you will find your power.

So, the technique to find your miracle, is to find why you have come to Earth. Here is the simple technique to find this mission.

Ask yourself what have you done in your life that you really loved and felt most alive doing? This is a clue as to what you have come to Earth to do.

Ask yourself what you have done on Earth that made you feel false, empty and less energetic? What makes you feel tired? This is your illusion in life, not your mission but rather your distraction from your true mission.

One great way to find your mission, is to find exactly what it is that bothers you in life, your biggest problem. Behind this problem is your mission.

So, when you discover this mission you will begin your miracle journey. Just lean into it and begin it.

God bless.

Exercise

1. **Acting Warm Up:**

   This is not an easy warm up but it is an effective way to open your throat chakra and begin to channel vocally. Do this exercise at least once to see if it helps open you up to vocal channeling.

   a. Google: "Free actor monologues." Find one you like, with strong emotional content. Begin to read it aloud, as if you were the person in the monologue. Find one that is as intensely emotional as you can stand and really try to express that emotion. Within a few tries you will begin to flow in the emotions of the person in the monologue. When you reach this point you are channeling.

2. **More Channeling:**

   Do the "Meditation to Meet Your Guides," again. Keep in mind that no matter what you get, the information should be accepted as correct. Ask:

   a. How the people in your life today are important to your life purpose?

   b. Do you have a soul mate, or soul mates from other lifetimes that you know now?

   c. Will you meet other soul mates in the future, as yet unknown to you?

Chapter 4: Channeling Past Lives From Akashic Records

When you become a fluent channeler, you are accessing the Akashic Records, or collective unconscious, without even realizing it. This chapter will formally introduce you to the Akashic Records, so that you will further develop your ability to be a channel for all knowledge.

What are the Akashic records?

1. Contain all knowledge of human and non-human experience.

2. Automatically accessed when you are channeling.

3. Contain all the birth, life and death information of every soul in the human realm and every being in the universe.

4. Contain the history of the cosmos.

5. Exist in a non-physical source.

6. Sometimes called the "Mind of God," "Book of Life," Universal Computer," "Collective Unconscious," "Hall of Records," etc.

7. Can be used to review:

   - Your soul purpose

   - Past and future lives

   - Karmic relationships

   - Your life's blocks and obstacles

- Why we relive same dramas and negative patterns
- How to change your luck
- What natural gifts and talents you are meant to express in this lifetime
- Who you are at a soul level
8. Updated automatically.

Ways to access the Akashic Records

1. Astral projection.
2. Channeling Spirit in deep hypnotic trance. We will use this method.

Akashic Records are reviewed prior to being born, to plan your life.

1. They are reviewed so you can plan a life on Earth, which will set up soul contract for evolving.
2. The family and body you choose are made to support this contract.
3. We are all born with "birth amnesia," to help learn our lessons without knowing what they are and why we are doing what we do.

Notable books about the Akashic Records

- "Journey of Souls," "Destiny of Souls" and "Evidence of Life Between Lives," by Michael Newton, a hypnotherapist who has worked with subjects in deep states, has many accounts of the akashic record, or "Book of Life."
- "Man: How, Whence, and Whither?" by C. W. Leadbeater

(clairvoyant). The book records the history of Atlantis , other civilizations and the future of earth in the 28th century.[2]

- "How to Read Akashic Records," by Linda Howe

- "The Law of One, Book I," a book purported to contain conversations with a channeled "social memory complex," known to humans as, "Ra." This book states that Edgar Cayce received his information from the Akashic records. "We have explained before, that the intelligent infinity is brought into intelligent energy, from eighth density or octave. The one sound vibratory complex called, "Edgar" used this gateway to view the present, which is not the continuum you experience but the potential social memory complex of this planetary sphere. The term your peoples have used for this is the "Akashic Record," or the "Hall of Records."

Preparation to Read The Akashic Records

It is advisable to do a preparatory exercise, one that will develop your ability to visualize scenes and stories, as well as help you choose a time from the past, which attracts you. This historical time usually attracts you because it is relevant to your current lifetime.

Preparation Exercise to Read The Akashic Records

a. Prepare using a meditation from L-O-V-E formula in Chapter 1.

b. Review a list of events in history. As of writing of the book the Internet provides a very good summary list located at www.enotes.com/topics/world-history-ancient-through-early-modern-times.

c. Choose a time in history that feels familiar and interesting to you, that has always fascinated you. Perhaps this event was in Egypt, Rome or The middle Ages.

d. Now imagine you have entered that time and allow your mind to visualize a day dream about it.

Over time you will get better and better at this. At first it will feel like you are making it up. However, with practice channeling the information in the Akashic Records, will become more fluid and take on a life of its own.

Overview of How to Channel the Akashic Records.

The following steps are simply an overview of how to channel the Akashic Records. Following this overview is a picture to use to help you visualize what the Hall of Records might look like, the actual meditation in writing and a link to where it is recorded for your use.

After you have become good at visualization, you are ready to channel your Akashic Records. Here is a brief overview of the steps.

1. Review a list of events in history. As of writing of the book the Internet provides a very good summary list located at www.enotes.com/topics/world-history-ancient-through-early-modern-times.

a. Choose a time in history that feels familiar and interesting to you, that has always fascinated you as you did in the Visualization exercise above.

2. When you have done this continue with the L-O-V-E

formula:

a. Let go in meditation. Review the ways to theta trance from Chapter 1. It is imperative to properly channel the Akashic Records, to be in as deep a trance as possible, without falling asleep.

    i. You can buy a professional meditation aid to access the Akashic Records from a New Age retailer, if you feel you need help.

    ii. You can use the original channeled script to help you access the Akashic Records. It is included in the next section recorded for you. As well, you can record the words in it and use it as part of your preparatory meditation. If you use the script, you may skip the, "Open in prayer" and "Vibrational alignment" steps of the L-O-V-E formula, as they are contained within it.

b. Open in prayer. "Father, mother, god, all spirits of highest light and love, allow me to access the Akashic records for myself or 'name.' My full name is __. My date of birth is ____. Allow all information about my soul's past and future to be received accurately, with validated evidence and healing, as intended for highest good and benefit of all. Amen. "

c. Vibrationally align with the Great Hall of Records. Imagine a great building, (picture below) with high white stone pillars, which looks like a temple in ancient Greece, or Rome. This is the Akashic record hall. All the knowledge of the entire universe and everything about you, exists inside.

d. Entirely receive.

3. As you drift inside the Akashic Record Hall, you see endless rows of books. Recite your name and date of birth. Then, ask to be shown the book for your soul.

4. Ask the Akashic records to show you the lifetime that is most important in your past, to this lifetime. Feel yourself shift into a dream sequence, channeling that lifetime in great detail.

5. Ask what it is you are supposed to be doing in this lifetime, to compliment that lifetime.

6. You can use the Akashic records to see your future, the past, see the outcome of an event, heal an aspect of yourself or know your life purpose. All you have to do, is ask when you are in the Akashic Library.

7. When you are done, record everything you learned. The more you do this, the more you will learn about yourself and your life.

Use This Picture To Help Visualize and Align With The Great Hall Of Records

Guided Meditation To The Akashic Records (Channeled)

After doing a theta meditation, as outlined in the L-O-V-E formula explained in Chapter 1, to relax, you can read this script to gain access to the Akashic Records. You may enter the records as often as you like to get answers to life questions.

The following meditation is recorded for you at this link. www.spiritmediumlaura.com/akashicmeditation.wma

If you would like to record your own version of this meditation you can do so very simply on your computer. Go here to read how: www.wikihow.com/Record-Your-Voice-on-a-Computer

Guided Meditation To The Akashic Records

Slowly open and close your eyes ten times, while focusing on an object in front of you. With each open and close, remind yourself how deeply relaxed you are getting.

Begin by imagining you are a little speck of light, looking at your body asleep in your bed. It is midnight and all is quiet.

Your body is meaningless to you. It is only an empty vessel.

Suddenly, without warning, you start to feel a pull. Your mind is now being pulled towards the window in your bedroom, out into the starry sky.

You follow it. You look down at the houses. They are getting smaller below you. It is a dark night but the stars in the sky are glowing and pulling you towards them, with a divine awareness and consciousness.

You are not frightened. You see everything in a new way, as if all the colors, the light, the sound and the temperature are more than what they are. You experience everything as if it is healing, multi-dimensional and possessing of a wise consciousness. Even the air is glowing.

You think this is what it must feel like to permanently leave your physical life, on Earth. You start to see things like a bird but a bird from God, with a new perception.

You continue to be pulled upwards and out of the Earth's atmosphere.

Suddenly, you decide to look back. You look down on Earth. It is a beautiful large ball of green, blue and white colors. You are happy and content and light. You have no fear, no concerns and feel very, very free.

The force field continues to tug at you. As you turn around, off in the distance you see a gorgeous castle in the sky, on a huge mountain of clouds. You believe this must be heaven, or a place of supernatural powers. You gladly move closer.

As you approach this mountain of clouds, you start to hear music. However, it is indescribable, for just like what you saw earlier, it is multidimensional and extremely beautiful.

You are ecstatic. The sounds are miraculous, healing and move you in positive, new emotional ways. It is as if the sounds you are hearing are developing your sense of God and all the magnificence and love that go with the concept.

The lights ahead continue to flicker. It is like the aurora borealis but with multi-dimensional, indescribable colors and feeling.

You have arrived.

As you enter this kingdom, a large gate opens.

Immediately, two Angels greet you, one on each side of you.

You notice they are taking your hands. You no longer are just a ball of light, now you have a body, albeit one of energy but a body, nevertheless.

They lead you to a great hall, off in the distance.

As you get to the hall, they introduce you to an ancient but pleasant looking person. This is the keeper of the Hall of Akashic Records. He is a spiritual guide, here to assist you in learning their mysteries.

He asks, "Why are you here?"

"To view my records," you say. He looks very pleased as if he is happy you have asked.

"It is good," he says "that you see your records. It will help with your life on Earth. Come this way." With a quick gesture he leads you into the great hall.

Inside it looks like the hall never ends. Row upon row of books, extend infinitely into space. You are just a tiny speck in its magnificence - and rightly so. You feel this is how it should be for you, to be small within the hall.

He says, "Follow me." You do with great speed.

Finally, after what seems to be an eternity of turns and lifts and corridors, he finally gets you to your book.

"There it is," he says. You look upon it with instant glee. This is your book, the book of your soul.

But something is wrong! Your name is not on this book. Instead, a design is on it, strange and beautiful.

You look at the keeper and ask, "Does this design mean anything?"

He smiles kindly, as if he knows. "This is your soul name. It is your essence name. Call upon it anytime you want to know something about yourself that is deep, hidden and personal. Your soul name will reveal your truth. It is sacred, like a secret code which unlocks your power."

You look at the name, but it is something you do not know how to pronounce, or say. It appears as a three dimensional design, glowing in gold.

You ask, "Would you pronounce it for me?"

The keeper says, "Yes." Immediately and with great alacrity he repeats your name.

He repeats it again and then one more time, even more slowly. You try to repeat what he said. You cannot.

"Listen again." He says it even more slowly.

It sounds like nothing you have ever heard before, just like the music outside was unfamiliar but pleasing and extremely beautiful.

"Say it again," you ask. He does and you realize what it sounds like. You hear it like a unique iteration of sounds from nature, or something similar: a gurgling brook, a crashing ocean wave, the coo of an owl, the wind in the pine trees, a warm crackling fire, the echo of the wind in a cavern, or something else.....

It is difficult to pronounce, but now you can at least have something to remember it by. You keep that thought in your mind for the future, to remember and draw upon its power.

The keeper gives you some last minute instructions.

"Just ask the book what you want to know and the book will take you there. This is very easy. The book is intelligent and will respond to your instructions. I am going to go now," he says.

You are a little scared to be left alone with this supernatural book, but you accept he is leaving. Once alone you start by asking the book, "Please open to the page with the lifetime I need to know related to the lifetime I am now experiencing."

The book immediately responds. The pages flip open to the right location.

On it is a picture of something that looks very familiar. It is a moving picture, like a film and you ask to see this in greater detail. The book accommodates you and suddenly, you are catapulted into the movie.

You look about.

What do you see? Are you in a rural or urban area?

What time in history are you in? Are you in the distant or near past? Are you male or female?

Look down at your feet. Are you wearing shoes? If so, what type?

How old are you?

What are you doing?

Now be quiet. Think about your life on earth and a question you have. Something very important is about to be revealed to you, related to a current life crisis, decision or direction you need. Listen up and pay attention. Just be silent and receive. Allow a story to unfold before you.

Take as long as you need.

Good. Now that your story is over, you ask the book to close and telepathically you call to the Keeper to come for you. You do not have to wait long. He appears almost instantaneously.

You ask to be led out of the hall back to your Angel Guides. He complies and says, "Fair well."

He reminds you, "The information you were given is sacred and important. Remember it often and use it. It is an honor to have received it."

You say, "Thank you" and turn to leave.

The angels are waiting there with great joy and love. They come to either side of you and escort you back to the gate of the kingdom of the Great Hall of Records.

You say, "Good bye," and turn to leave.

As soon as you leave the gates, you again become a speck of light and are drawn, meteorically towards Earth. Before you have experienced anything, you are placed back into your body and are awakened.

This was a very interesting journey. You now record what you saw and learned.

Exercises

1. **Dance To Trance Warm Up.**

   Following the LOVE formula revealed in Chapter 1, you will need to start with a meditation of some sort to begin.

   Find some beautiful hypnotic meditation music to play. I have found beautiful meditation music on www.youtube.com.

   Now close your eyes as you stand and listen to the music. Immerse your entire body into the feeling of the music, move along with it in any way you feel. The more you move the easier it will be to channel, so really abandon yourself to your feelings.

   Channeling is about letting go and letting the messages flow through you.

2. **Channeling Akashic Records.**

   Do the Akashic Records Guided Meditation described earlier in this chapter. It is recorded for you at this link. www.spiritmediumlaura.com/akashicmeditation.wma

   When you are through, take a moment to remain in a calm, centered state.

   - Ask your Spiritual Guides to channel through you the importance of the past life you just saw. You might want to record what comes through, as you will be in a trance state and will have difficulty recalling it completely.

   - Ask your guides what you can do in this lifetime to complete your purpose.

   "Channeling Spirits" – Page 68

- Ask your guides what soul contracts you have with others in this lifetime, which you must heal.

3. **Channel the Akashic Records for a friend or client.**

Prepare with the LOVE Formula.

- Let Go: Get into a relaxed and calm state using a meditation you like from Youtube, Dance to Trance, Intuitive Drawing or the acting monologue described in the prior chapter.

- Open in prayer. Use this prayer to begin your session with a client or friend. "Father, mother, god, all spirits of highest light and love, allow me to access the akashic records for the full name of ____. The date of birth is ___. Allow all information about this soul's past and future, to be received accurately with validated evidence and healing, as intended for highest good and benefit of all. Amen. "

- Vibrationally align with the Great Hall of Records. Imagine a great building (picture earlier in this chapter) with high white stone pillars, which looks like a temple in ancient Greece or Rome. This is the Akashic Record Hall. All the knowledge of the entire universe exists inside.

- Entirely receive.

As you drift inside the Akashic Record Hall, you see endless rows of books. Mentally recite your friend or client's name and date of birth again and ask to be shown the book for their soul.

Ask the Akashic records to show you the lifetime which is most important in their past, to this lifetime. Feel yourself shift into a dream like state, receiving from that lifetime in great detail. Channel vocally what you are seeing, feeling or hearing. Whatever you get is correct. Be sure to record your words.

Ask what they are supposed to be doing in this lifetime, to compliment that lifetime.

Conclusion

I want to thank you for sharing this exciting journey with me. Hopefully, you have discovered through this book that Channeling is not a mystery. It can be developed with scientific precision.

Look to my website: www.SpiritMediumLaura.com for continued material and classes.

Here are some planned or already finished. They are already published or will be on www.Amazon.com.

If they are not yet available on Amazon then they exist as e-books on my website, www.SpiritMediumLaura.com. If you have difficulty finding email me for assistance at Laura@SpiritMediumLaura.com.

Manifesting Magic: The Soul Abundance Law of Attraction Secret. Available on www.Amazon.com as of publishing of this book.

Intuitive living is the secret to luck, synchronicities, hunches, guidance and success. If you are looking to improve your ability to manifest your dreams, this book will provide a simple, yet powerful plan to activate the your real magic of your soul.

Psychic Creativity.

Learn how to use psychometry, see and read auras using a unique system spirit channeled to me, read and do mind body soul healing using chakras, read billets, do telepathy, medical scanning and remote viewing.

Psychic Mediumship.

Learn how to speak to loved ones in spirit the natural way. This fun, spiritual and divine book includes opening the natural way, getting details from a soul in spirit, how to be a psychic detective and sending souls into the light. This is for the more advanced student who has mastered their psychic senses.

Holistic Business Success.

You can do the work of your dreams and earn a great living at it. This book contains a complete holistic business marketing plan.

Contact

Please feel free to call upon me, Laura Bartolini Mendelsohn, for readings, or coaching in any of these areas. I can be reached by phone at (954) 465-7338 or email at Laura@SpiritMediumLaura.com

My website is loaded with testimonials and information to learn more about me.

Much love and many blessings,

Spirit Medium Laura

www.SpiritMediumLaura.com

(954) 465-7338

FREE BONUS

Get FREE "Channeling Spirit" Video Class Intro by joining mailing list at <u>www.SpiritMediumLaura.com</u>

Made in the USA
Las Vegas, NV
11 July 2022

51398577R00052